GRAND TREACHERIES, LITTLE RESPITES

ANNIKA

I dedicate this poetry collection to my former innocent self.

-Annika

Follow me on Instagram, @annika_poetry

Contents

1. When Life Makes You Forlorn 1
2. You Will Never Leave Her 2
3. Cerulean Blue 3
4. What Is Poetry? 4
5. On Crippling Anxiety 5
6. She's A Madonna 7
7. Clean Glass 8
8. A Calm Serene Lake 9
9. Crown Of Love 10
10. Fizz! 11
11. Our Hotel Lobby 12
12. I Believed Once 13
13. Her Moon 14
14. My Idea Of Romance 15
15. Her 16
16. I Am In Love With You 17
17. I Am Home Now 18
18. Creator And His Creation 19
19. I Know Not 20
20. Turquoise Tribe 21
21. Adventure 22
22. If God Be An Author 23
23. Being A Poet 24
24. Summer 25

Contents

25. Anthem 26

26. Making A Hope List 27

27. Poetry And Comfort 28

28. Her Life 29

29. Bridges Burned 30

30. A Not So Profound Poem On Death 31

31. I Carry On 32

32. I Can Carry On… 33

33. Explanations And Me 34

34. Being True 35

35. Eyes Are Gateways 36

36. In The Kingdom Of God 37

37. On Friendship 38

38. A Devil Unknown (depression) 39

39. Mirrors 40

40. I Don't Sleep… 41

41. Mirrors And The Truth 42

42. A Lover's Strain 43

43. A Mother To Her Child 44

44. Taking Things To The Grave 45

45. Remembrance 46

46. Mother! 47

47. Poetry And Me 48

48. Now 49

Contents

49. Crayons And Life 50

50. A Reader Forever! 51

51. A Lover's Value 52

52. Love And Adventure 53

1. When life makes you forlorn

When life makes you forlorn
What do you do?

I think of you
Your love makes me new

ANNIKA

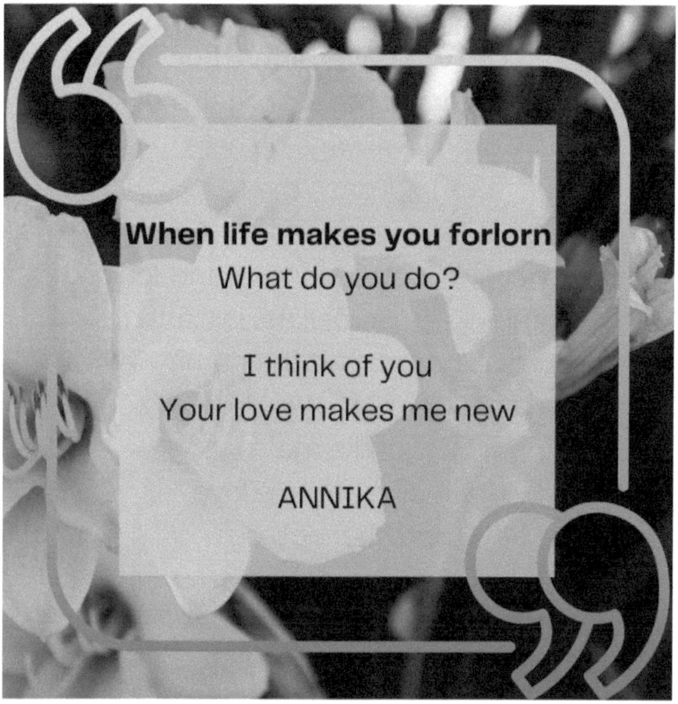

2. You Will Never Leave Her

You will never leave her
yet you will never forget me
you will always be hers
but I will pass the test

For whenever you hear 'love' and 'longing'
you will remember me instantly
but she has played the game well
and shed tears that you could see
unlike me
I will always have love
and she, victory

ANNIKA

3. Cerulean Blue

I am cynical and Cerulean Blue.
Blue is the colour of love, some say.
Conflicting are my emotions
so is the definition of my life.

ANNIKA

4. What is Poetry?

What is Poetry?

Poetry
has not got much to do
with literacy,
It's more about having an
artistic bone in your body
and having decency

It's the language of the
mind
made up of thoughts,
feelings and experiences
of more than just one's
body

Poetry
is telling the story
of one's loss; colossal loss
when maybe it should
have been a
hands down victory

But it has to be a well told
story...

ANNIKA

5. On Crippling Anxiety

On Crippling Anxiety

There are certain big moments in life
when nobody will fight for you
and you must do it all by yourself
you don't need wisdom
to identify this particular
situation, when you're in it, per se
just basic awareness and honesty
and a will to win no matter what
even though the path to victory
may seem cruel and petty
and a sound notion of self-interest

But that's where I flounder
Anxiety gets the better of me
Anxiety gets in the way
Anxiety needs to be kept at bay
I put on a poor show because of it
there is struggle without,
that needs to be conquered
and I get drowned in
the strife within me
the final outcome is
you guessed it right, a tragedy

ANNIKA

6. She's a Madonna

She's a Madonna

The Moon and the stars
she encompasses them all
Silver and Gold jewellery
beautiful, adorned with filigree
she owns them, wears them, carelessly
huge mirrors for her
to reflect her beauty
to be admired
for eternity
The night is hers
and so is the day
she is a Madonna
and he can't endure it
if she is away

ANNIKA

7. Clean Glass

Clean Glass
Window pane
Slanting rain
across it

Look through it
It's all gorgeous Green
with colourful flowers
dancing

I sit within
the coffee house
sipping through a hot cup
enjoying a book and
my individual rain

ANNIKA

8. A Calm Serene Lake

A
Calm serene lake
Blue water
A Pink blooming lotus
It's Green waxy leaves
I throw a White pebble in
Plop! The sound of water
The ripples in the lake
...followed by
magical tranquillity

Annika

11. Our Hotel Lobby

Our Hotel Lobby

I walk past the lobby
of the hotel
Where we used to sneak
out
in the middle of work,
to make out
both of us
minimum wage; lowest of
the low
workers, in-love

Now it looks deserted

The lobby misses us
It lacks us
it calls out for us
but you are not here
and I alone am not enough

ANNIKA

12. I Believed Once

I believed that there was meaning
to one's suffering
turns out even the Gods can turn
and let their promises burn

ANNIKA

13. Her Moon

Her Moon

The moon is hers
she wears it as her anklet
it shines ever so brightly
when she walks, when she moves
emanating a Silver light

ANNIKA

14. My Idea Of Romance

My idea of romance
begins with you
and ends with you
a burning cigarette
in your hand
you're standing
at the gate of the factory
in evenings made of
Grey sky and the
Pink fading Sun
the smell of that scene
fills the city
and my heart

Annika

15. Her

Her

She could never
bring herself to return
citing 'unwanted' purchase reason
a wrong item
imagine her tragedy
when she
had to get rid
of her unwanted, own
flesh and blood

ANNIKA

16. I Am In Love With You

I am in love with you
you know that
You are my bad addiction
you know that
Can't get rid of you
you know that
Gotta kick you out
Wanna kick you out
Will relish life, only then
you know that
But then I think
what's life without
one bad addiction
you know that
ANNIKA

17. I Am Home Now

I have walked for a thousand years
in a dessert on hot golden sand
under the bright Yellow scorching Sun
now I have finally found
the coolest shade under the greenest tree
now I am not so forlorn
I rest under it
my body calm
my heart
singing a psalm
now I have come home
I am finally home now

ANNIKA

18. Creator and his Creation

If I create you
Do I own you?
Do I own you
Wholly and completely?
Never letting you go...?

But you have a throbbing heart
A life of your own
You live gracefully
All by yourself

I will shine proudly in your dazzling brightness
A dazzling brightness
For the world to see...
Your pain is mine
my happiness is yours
Live wondrously
O creation of mine!

If you shine
I feel bright
If you laugh
I will smile

I can't let you go
Because you were never mine

What's inside of you
Struggles to come out
When it does
It's beautiful but painful
But it's not yours any more

Let go creator
You are not in control
Any more...

ANNIKA

19. I Know Not

I know not

Live life to the fullest
Life is short

You want happiness
Do you not?

You want only happiness
Do you not?

Can one only be happy?
I know not

Can sorrow be reduced
No matter what?

ANNIKA

20. Turquoise Tribe

Turquoise Tribe

Where is my Turquoise tribe?
I long for it oh so dearly!
Where are my people
With whom I vibe
Where is that promised land?
My slice of a colourful life!

AnniKa

21. Adventure

She was never loved
Never someone's
heart and all
No matter where she went
Her fate followed her after all

She lived and died hated
No matter what she did
She was never understood
A tragedy she lived

ANNIKA

22. If God be an author

If God be an author
And life poetry
Be ready for both
Happiness
And tragedy

ANNIKA

25. Anthem

I could never sing to this tune that
'You only live once'
Have as much fun as
You want now
Who knows what
Will happen tomorrow

This was always my anthem
We have not one life
We do come back though
Over and over again
To correct our mistakes
Going through the same pain
Till divinity, we do attain!

26. Making a Hope list

Make a list
Of everything
That fills you
With hope

Read it out aloud
every time
You are about to
mope
Let the list include
Baths with hot water
And scented soap

Include spending time
with your
Favourite pup
Or your hobby
Or getting a
Massage foot rub

It could be books
Reading which
Transports you to
another world
Or just eating
Your favourite
Meatball sub

Make a list of
Everything that
Fills you with hope

Read it out loud
Every time
You are
About to mope

27. Poetry and comfort

I find comfort
Deep and intense,
In poetry

Oh, wonderful poets,
with your creations

What would I do
Without thee?

ANNIKA

28. Her Life

Her Life

She knew it could all end in tragedy
Yet she took the first step
To cross the big blue sea
Do not judge her too harshly
All she wanted was to be free

She had nothing; no one
And no money
No plan no sweetheart
And no honey

ANNIKA

29. Bridges burned

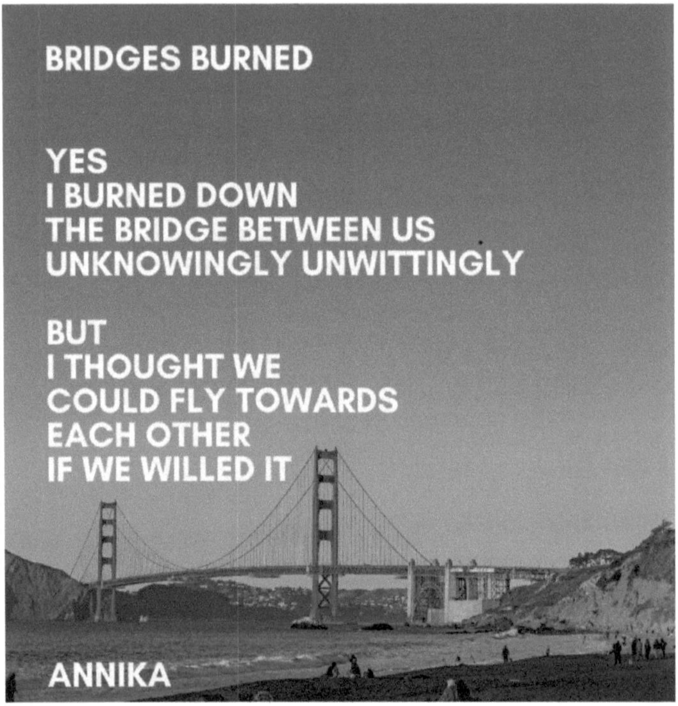

BRIDGES BURNED

YES
I BURNED DOWN
THE BRIDGE BETWEEN US
UNKNOWINGLY UNWITTINGLY

BUT
I THOUGHT WE
COULD FLY TOWARDS
EACH OTHER
IF WE WILLED IT

ANNIKA

30. A not so profound poem on Death

Death is silence
Resounding, utter, absolute
Silence inside and out
Silence within and without

Death is the solution
The final solution
For the malady of life
The most powerful tincture
For your soul
To make it whole
To seal the cracks
To erase the bruises
To nurse the blood-filled cuts
Of your soul
To make it whole

They say there is an afterlife
There is a point
Beyond death
Past which
You live again
So don't die in vain
Enjoy the pain
And the journey
Take your favourite blanket
To the coffin
Sleep there
Peacefully
Better than a baby
In your warm blanky
Till the slate is all clear
Till you begin again

ANNIKA

31. I Carry On

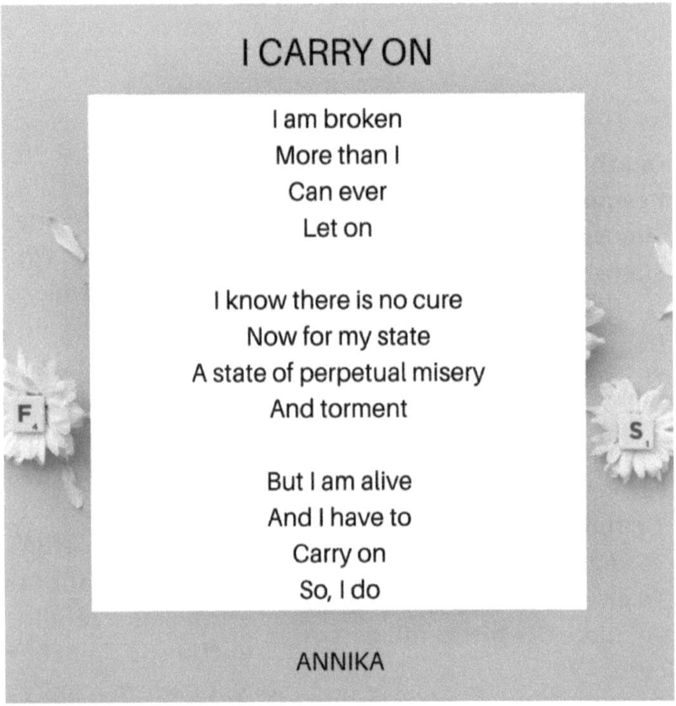

I CARRY ON

I am broken
More than I
Can ever
Let on

I know there is no cure
Now for my state
A state of perpetual misery
And torment

But I am alive
And I have to
Carry on
So, I do

ANNIKA

32. I Can Carry On…

I Can Carry On

What I'll always have
Is my unadulterated
Pure gold
Good intent
A malice less attitude
A God given talent

To shine through
Life without
Succumbing to
Total darkness
For the rest
Of my life
Now…

ANNIKA

33. Explanations and Me

Explanations and me

The more I try
To explain myself
The more
Misunderstood
I become

That's when I realize
It isn't just them
Against me
It is me against me

It was always
Out of my hands
You see...

ANNIKA

34. Being True

Being True

I lie to get the world
And speak verily
To get
The Almighty

ANNIKA

35. Eyes are Gateways

EYES ARE GATEWAYS

MY EYES WERE THE REAL
CULPRITS
THEY LET YOU IN
STRAIGHT TO MY HEART
WITHOUT MY PERMISSION
THE BETRAYERS...

ANNIKA

36. In the Kingdom of God

I am but a beggar
In the kingdom of God
Hoping to be bestowed upon
By eternal love as alms

Keep me in your prayers
For my wait to be memorable
And for what comes after
To be-Spectacular!

ANNIKA

37. On Friendship

On Friendship

I haven't made any new friend recently
"You should mingle more"
"You should share more"
I will be blamed for my plight, surely
Schools teach History and Geography
Can they instil honesty?

ANNIKA

38. A Devil Unknown (Depression)

A Devil Unknown (Depression)

Time trickles away
Seconds turning into minutes
And minutes turning into hours
And to me
Within that time span
Opening and shutting of an eyelid
Seems like a life span
Seems like some unknown
yet familiar devil
has possessed my soul
it has taken my brain hostage
making it fatigued
torn and lacerated
painful and heavy
like a very pregnant belly
the throbbing constantly
of my brain
does not stop
seems like a deadly ailment
(Could it be?)
I am in an endless hurry...

ANNIKA

39. Mirrors

MIRRORS

WAS IT LOVE?
I NEVER KNEW

BUT WHEN I LOOK
INTO THE MIRROR
STILL, I SEE YOU

ANNIKA

40. I Don't Sleep…

I Don't Sleep

I can never forget
I remember everything
Every colour,
Every word
And every shadow
When they ask me
I don't tell
How far down
In my life I fell
I don't sleep to rest
I sleep-only hoping to
Forget

ANNIKA

41. Mirrors and the Truth

MIRRORS AND THE TRUTH

They say mirrors
Tell only the truth
I stopped looking
Into the mirror
Because it always
Shows me, you!

ANNIKA

42. A Lover's Strain

A lover's strain

My scream
Will tear apart your
Beautiful Dream...
...when you are
Calm and peaceful
Taking away your
Tranquility
Leaving you helpless...
You will want to move
To do something
To stop your heart
From burning
So incredibly
But in vain...

I will have offended you
Permanently
After you
Cease to live
Cease to breathe
In your final dark
underground crib...

ANNIKA

43. A mother to her child

The twinkle in your eye
Shines brightly...
As if it is the brightest
Star in the sky
It fills my heart
With hope and joy!

ANNIKA

44. Taking things to the grave

Taking Things to the Grave

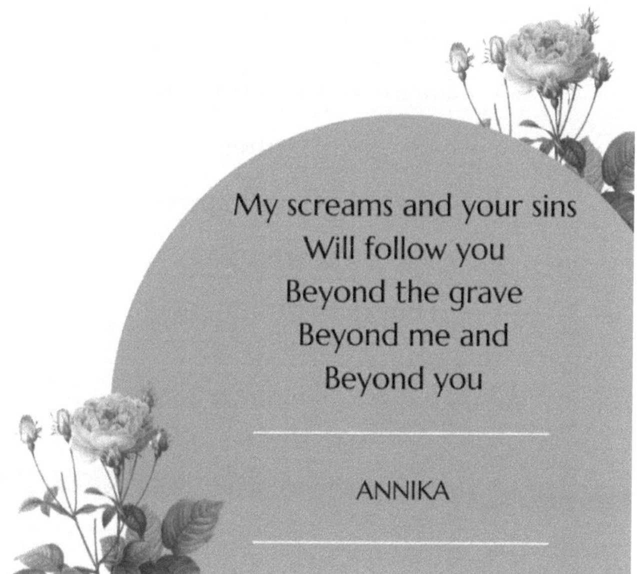

45. Remembrance

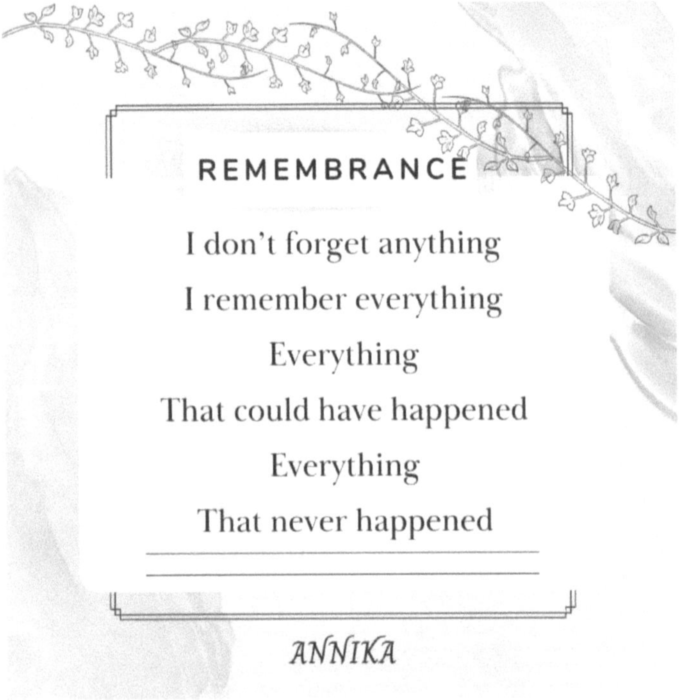

REMEMBRANCE

I don't forget anything
I remember everything
Everything
That could have happened
Everything
That never happened

ANNIKA

46. Mother!

Mother!
All that I have ever
Known of mother
Was her hunger
Always fending for money
Always fighting failure
Having to forgo pleasure
Forced into being
A mortal meagre
From an artist of
great calibre
Braving everyday
Plowing through chores
Trying to keep self-
calm
In the all pervasive
Misery and pain
Life is a tragedy
That cannot be slain!
Death treated her far
better than
life ever could
Death's deadly snare
could not match
Life's menacing scare
She is gone now
Beyond all the pain
She will never ever
Be hungry again!
ANNIKA

47. Poetry and me

POETRY AND ME

Bottled emotions...
Repressed memories...
All the insults gulped

Of denied entries
into the happinesses
of the world...

It all comes to me now
Untimely, uninvited and ugly
Now I burst into Poetry...

Annika

48. Now

NOW

Now
If you leave me
You will never be happy
Not for a second
Not for eternity

ANNIKA

49. Crayons and Life

CRAYONS AND LIFE

Crayons are brittle
Their words, strong

Crayons are colorful
But brittle
The words you write
With them
Are forever
Carved on paper
Like life

Life is brittle
It's meaning strong

ANNIKA

50. A Reader Forever!

A Reader Forever!

For there is no better joy
than turning day into night
And night into day
Getting lost into a storybook

Let the world come to an end
And time to a standstill
I will be peering unto
Stories of the adventurer who has set sail

A forever reader I will be
A forever joyful life will I lead!

ANNIKA

51. A Lover's Value

A Lover's Value

You fill my silent spaces
You soften my heart's creases
You brighten my days
and fill my dreams
with beautiful colours
You diffuse unnecessary noises
And loud judgements
that do not come
From without always

ANNIKA

52. Love and Adventure

Love and Adventure

What is love?
What is life?
Is it real?
...full of strife...

Love is pain
Life is a struggle
Neither is easy; it kills you;
Don't be deferential

A promising adventure
Turns bad; goes sour
A glorious path
Turns to sorrow and rubble

ANNIKA

THANK YOU!
THE END!

9 798887 728650

Printed by Libri Plureos GmbH in Hamburg,
Germany